RESURRECTION PIE

RESURRECTION PIE

JOHN WALL BARGER

LOUISIANA STATE UNIVERSITY PRESS ▌▌ BATON ROUGE

Published by Louisiana State University Press
lsupress.org

LSU Press Paperback Original

DESIGNER: Emily A. Olson
TYPEFACES: Cassia, text; Modula OT Tall, Magno Sans Variable, display

Cover photo: Flickr/"Project 365 #61: 020314 Vanishing Point" by Pete

LIBRARY OF CONGRESS CATALOGING-IN-PUBLICATION DATA

Names: Barger, John Wall, 1969–, author
Title: Resurrection pie / John Wall Barger.
Other titles: Resurrection pie (Compilation)
Description: Baton Rouge: Louisiana State University Press, 2026.
Identifiers: LCCN 2025045760 (print) | LCCN 2025045761 (ebook) | ISBN 978-0-
    8071-8606-0 (paperback) | ISBN 978-0-8071-8687-9 (epub) | ISBN 978-0-8071-
    8688-6 (pdf)
Subjects: LCGFT: Poetry
Classification: LCC PR9199.4.B365 R48 2026 (print) | LCC PR9199.4.B365 (ebook)
LC record available at https://lccn.loc.gov/2025045760
LC ebook record available at https://lccn.loc.gov/2025045761

The house was full of sounds... They came in
to her with a quality of awakening, resurgence,
as though the house itself had been asleep.

—FAULKNER, *SANCTUARY*

If only I could
Make you hear
The sound of snow
Falling late at night
At the old temple
In the forest of Shinoda!

—HAKUIN

CONTENTS

RESURRECTION PIE

The Ridges on the Cerebral Surface of the Brain Are Called *Gyri*

The black hole whirlpool
   Van Gogh painted
over Saint-Rémy-de-Provence.
   Its violent winds,
its quiet heart.

O my soul,
   out the asylum window
wheels in wheels
   roll by themselves,
you carnivorous birds.

Sky a pinwheel
   at a child's memorial.
O my soul, I am close.
   This night
I may be required of you.

I

Invocation

for Barbudo, Jocinero, Bailador, Pocapena, Granadino,
Islero, Avispado, Burlero…

The bulls that gored matadors feint as one,
scythes in the dark, as if upon a raft
that comes apart beneath them
in the rapids and they fall,
a drunken brawl of rolling eyes,
mariachis strumming behind us.
August 28, 1947, Islero gores
the most famous toreador on earth.
They cut and cut the bull,
prodding, hacking him at the nape,
he reels, falls, they wipe knives
on his fur and drag the corpse off
on a chariot like some B-movie god.
May 16, 1920, Bailador drools
black string, inhaling deeply
our cigars, dreaming he's a dervish,
a starveling, a double-barreled shotgun
or a dope fiend in a Ginsberg poem,
wearing a sleazy grin and riding out of town
on a Triumph motorcycle with three
goats on the back in a cage.
We toss our hats after him, "Hoy!"

The Saboteurs

Soon we didn't even hear the explosions. We strolled past each new crater as if it had always been there. Nobody knew the saboteurs' agenda. No demands, no manifesto. Explosions were *green*. "How," barked a general, "do they make them *green?*" Their targets seemed indiscriminate: hospital, lake, bank, parking lot, forest. And they, the saboteurs, seemed invisible. Trackless. Explosions just happened. Now and then a drunk or a child voiced what we'd all been thinking: that maybe, somehow, our city had been lined with bombs before any of us were born. That there were no saboteurs.

By dumb luck, we captured one. Green-eyed, calm. Unremarkable. We starved and stretched him. Thumbscrewed him. Ground his face against our maps, demanding names, plans, dates, *anything*. He was the gentlest man I'd ever met. He kept blessing us and our families. We wept as we hurt him. To each other we called him Francis. In a circle among us, his torturers, Francis said, "I am sorry, I do not understand your questions. But aren't the bombs sublime?" "How?" we asked, sincerely. He just smiled.

We received orders, drove Francis to a field. He bowed to us in the grass. Felix drew the short straw. But Felix, instead of executing Francis, offered his gun. We all handed Francis our guns. We left him there and drove back to our decimated city, unarmed.

No Longer Invited to Dinner

for the winners of the 2014 Darwin Award

Let us celebrate you,
Anastasia and Miguel, copulating on a balcony,
        falling six stories.

From birth we advised,
keep your things close, do not share,
        it's yours, all yours.

We were fools. Perhaps now
you are rocks falling into an abyss
        for one hundred years.

Does it matter? Now all you had
is impounded. As if it were never yours!
        Even the memories,

even the last: his erection in the dark.
Even your unpaid parking tickets.
        Even those crates

of unread books in your parents' attic.
Even the possum in your garden
        you never mentioned to anyone.

We're all teenagers, stoned,
horny, stepping out of the party. Praise us all!
        Cut loose our strings.

We told you *we* were the teachers, *this*
the class. It's all for the good, we said,
        hoping you would make it so.

Now look what happened:
you're no longer invited to dinner.
                    Even the good feeling

        you became the wall around. Miguel
hoisted Anastasia onto the railing.
                    Anastasia unzipped him.

        Let us giggle with them.
Let us make love to the air.
                    Like a Godard jump cut.

        Trick of bad editing.
That sound? A phone ringing.
                    Yes, it sounds close. It's not.

How I Learned to Sleepwalk

When I was a teenager
one of my parents' friends
told me, off the cuff,
I was good at analogies.
I was flattered. I wasn't good
at school, English,
or grammar—but *analogies*.

I'd always thought
lots of nonsense, of course.
Every boy does. But that
might be the moment
I gave myself permission
to think nonsense.

What do *you* do
with bizarre thoughts?
Do you let yourself
think "nonsense"?

Is there space in your garage
for mixed or indecorous
figures of speech that
don't mingle well with others?

If, after an afternoon nap,
"Toronto is a feral child"
pops into your head, do you retain it,
whatever is conjured by it,
hoping it will resurrect itself
later, on your nightly walk
beside the reservoir?

Or do you fling it away
as you would a prisoner
who won't confess
down ancient iron stairs
to the solitary confinement cells?

Where do you bury the dead?

They say great stories
have no secrets. But we humans
fly several kites at once.

I eat while sleeping.
I dance, work, love, sing
while sleeping.

I hunt the goblins that live
in the shadows
of the Forest of Clichés
while sleeping.

I fly several kites while sleeping.

Have I ever told you
you are good at analogies?

On your walk beside the reservoir
in the Dead Sea of the mind,
past the shark nets of the mind,
the Toronto child breaches

—an entire milieu out of the dark,
the harpoon of your attention
in her side, her eyes
three million lanterns flickering

and splashes
back into the water.

Rage Flowers

Poor miserable Louis
sat on my couch all afternoon,
head in his hands,
crying about his girlfriend, Li'l Pumpkin,
how she'd stolen his Ford Pinto
and left him.

Louis, bisected by evening light
angling from the window
on his left, was furious.
I never saw him so mad.

"When did she stop loving me?"
he blurted out. The madder he got,
the more he cried, writhing
in his seat, crumpling inward
like a burning house.

"The day," he murmured, theatrically,
"is too long, too slow.
I'm stuck in the freezing shadow
of the present moment."

"Nice phrase!" I said,
jotting it in my notebook.
Louis just kept crying,
repeating how old he feels,
how scary life will be
without Li'l Pumpkin in it.

That's when he started coughing
and coughing, his eyes bugging out.
I ran to get a glass of water.

When I came back
his lap was covered in blood!
Not blood, flower petals.

I blinked. Louis was coughing
red flower petals
onto his shirt, onto my couch.
From his lips
the petals drifted.

I picked up a handful
of the petals. So soft!
It was strange, as if I were
the first prehistoric creature
having the first dream.

Louis didn't seem to notice.
He kept repeating how mad he was,
now coughing whole flowers,
up to his knees in red petals,
coughing, coughing.

I called 911 and yelled into the phone:
"Please come quick! My friend
is knee-deep in soft flowers,
rising to his neck. It's so beautiful,
I don't know what to do!"

The Caretaker

A helmetless soldier
with a bellicose nose
knocked softly
on the innermost door
of the bunker.
His only job in the war:
care for the dictator's dog.
The dictator whispered
an order: Test *this* capsule
on the dog, now. The caretaker
blinked. The dictator
stared. So the caretaker
forced her muzzle open,
slipped the capsule in,
urged her jaws together,
breaking the glass.
The dog gazed at the dictator.
When sick, she always
placed her head on his lap.
She stepped toward him,
hiccupping. She fell, convulsing.
The dictator nodded.
At dawn the dictator's wife
swallowed a capsule
and he shot himself in the head.
The caretaker sat
upright. Was he the last?
He saw no one alive.
He moved through the bunker
slow, pulse echoing
in his cheekbones.
He followed orders.
First, he burned three bodies:

dictator, wife, dog.
Second, Luger in hand,
he gathered the puppies
from their cage.
Outside, bright morning.
The street wore a rubble gown,
ash ribbons in its hair.
He blinked. He once lived
just blocks away
with his wife.
Now it was April, not cold
but the puppies shivered.
One by one he lowered them
gently
to the black slash
where the garden had been.
They nosed in the ashes.
He lifted his favorite,
the girl that hopped
when he came in.
Pressing her on his face
on his ear
he spoke her name
her secret name
which nobody else knew.

Blossom Street

A room with all my favorite people
welcomes me with a cheer.
Dead ones are here, too.
I get a thumbs-up from
Uncle Mike. Matthew whispers
what a great poet I am.

I sit on the couch,
heart full, crying openly.
My favorite student,
who resembles a young
Vladimir I. Lenin,
tells me he loves me
like a brother.
As if demonstrating a trick,
he plucks a knife
out of the air
and slips the blade into my heart.

He speaks gently, eyes radiant:
Remove the blade, you'll bleed out,
better to leave it in,
enjoy the party for an hour.

I thank him
and walk the room,
slow, knife in my chest.

Others have knives
in their chests as well.
They nod as I pass.
Most cry with joy, as I do.
A few slump
like hobos in a play.

My friend the addict
bears an arrow through each palm.
He raises his hands
and asks, Haven't I lived warmly
and with sympathy?
Yes, yes, I say.
From outside, a muffled roar:
wingbeats, a spring storm.
I lie on the floor.

Here is all the love I deserve.
It is more than enough.
Some smile, nod off.
By now, each with a knife
in the heart. It's so late,
I shut my eyes.
Someone is holding my hand.

The roar of the storm
the only sound.

Resurrection Pie

When my sister died
my mother said,
Go to school, kid.
I would not. I asked
if a grave was dug
for me as well. She said
my body was wind
so where would she dig
a goddamn grave anyway?

I sat in my sister's room
with her flea circus
I'd said was *stupid*
so many times. One flea
pulled a fancy carriage.
One rode an old-timey
bike. With tweezers
I set each flea in place
and watched them
with a magnifying glass.
The tightrope walker
had its own box.
Why did my sister
draw dollar signs on the box?
I whispered to that flea,
I will not eat. Like fuck,
said my mother.

She left pie by the door.
I picked at it. Disgusting.
Stony crust, scaly layers,
gristle lumps, sinew strings,
fat. She'd made it
from old pies. I cursed it.

Still chewing,
I put on my sister's top hat,
hooked the tiny
pink umbrella to the flea.
The tightrope was elaborate:
twine stretched tight
between wee doll chairs
glued to chopsticks.
With shaky fingers
I lowered the flea
on the twine. It walked
an inch and flailed,
upside down. I nudged.
It kicked the air.

Her room was getting dark.
In the magnifying glass,
the flea was a dragon:
pink umbrella its flaming breath.
I stepped back.
Her construction
half in the closet
was a city.
It is the nature of cities
to glitter
to roar
so the rooftops glittered
so the funambulist
roared, speaking fire.

I released it.
It leapt off
into the red shag sea.

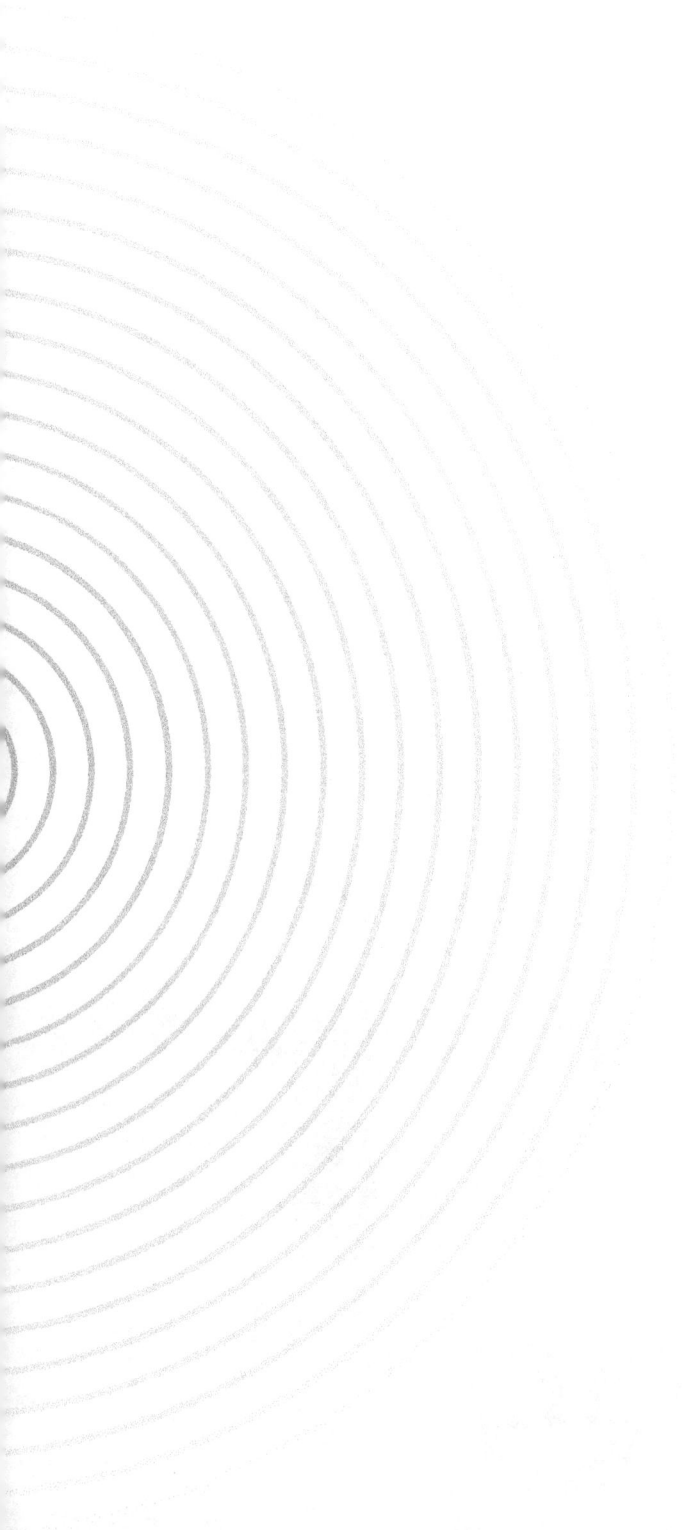

II

Lance Hardwood Proceeds to the Bardo Realms

I had a seizure on set.
There might have been
some blow involved.
Sandwiched between two
lovely young things
like a slice of ham;
sweaty faces, cameras,
barn door lights—
suddenly a lonesomeness
heavy as a gorilla on my chest.
I'd had it on good faith
I could stay on this earth.
Yet ... the chassis fell away.
I step out of the fur robe
of my belly, look back.
Lo, the fool I was. The carcass,
slack on a leather couch,
heavy in its pastures.
The famed "elephant trunk."
The mouth leaking last longings.
The mind still burbling
analogies: churning: cement mixer.
I seem to witness that mind
dissolve, white wine in the sea.
And then suddenly I am
other. Neither air nor water
but emptiness I am now
a symbol of. I turn.
The great mist clears upon
a shopping mall. Lions,
wing-rush. Skirling. Forms
inconceivable. Pleasures.
In arcades, under porticos.

Thereat my secret body like a grape
sweetens. I, queenless,
walk among my kind.
Seedspitters. Worshippers
of form. Among the gods
that eat. Gods eat the walls,
the trees. Tables, escalators.
Gods eat the young:
theirs, ours. Gods eat *us*
again, again, noisily.
Only silence, we tell ourselves,
can triumph. We crusade
for silence in our caves,
in silence. After an eternity,
silence eats the gods.

Their Beauty Was the Envy of the Neighborhood

I jimmied my neighbor's window, tossed the man over my shoulder and hauled him out the front door. A light breeze blew ashes across the lawn. A dark figure, bundle slung over his shoulder, crossed my path; I knew my own bed would be empty, my dear husband's spot still warm. Under the piano, my neighbor's husband hid, shivering. I pointed to the open door. I'd made my point. But he didn't go.

First few days he slept in the closet like a squirrel. It must have made him feel safe. I left a bowl of mixed nuts, gone in the morning. One night he scratched at my bedroom door, on all fours. I let him in. He grew on me. He came so hard I called him Euphrates. I decided he could stay. In his sleep he groaned, "I love you so much." "Who?" I said. "You," he groaned. "You who?" I said. "You," he groaned, and so on.

A scorpion climbed out of his mouth. It skittered off the bed, out the door, toward the baby's crib. Indeed, I'd underestimated my neighbor.

Border Ballad

I hop out of the VW hippie van
into a sieve of dust—ghost town, Arizona—holding hands
        with my parents. A bench,

    upturned nails: coffin boards, it looks like.
Grimy post office, long closed. Dad peers
        between fence slats, quietly. Dad,

    Dad, what're you lookin' at? China and India
often clash at Doklam, near Sikkim, where Tibet,
        India, and Bhutan intersect, a barren plateau

    scattered with glacial boulders, cosmic eggs
in desiccated grass. Dad doesn't say. I peek.
        Child your sick smile, says Franz Wright,

    is the border of sleep. Tarantulas:
a living pile. I am not awake when the cat jumps
        in the window, water rushing in a pipe,

    I'm running a fever, stomach plunging.
Chinese build a road, Indians camp there, and so on.
        If a coyote stalks your peripheral vision,

    does one recommend a doctor, priest,
or classics professor? I am awake but do not hear shots
        fired across disputed lands.

    One creature, the tarantulas, one loose wool sweater.
The dragon woke, death of the sun in its eyes.
        Every part of this poem a mistake,

the gentle sound of malicious agencies
crashing the amniotic membrane. How,
             asked Melville, can the prisoner reach outside

      except by thrusting through the wall?
I look and look between the slats. I wake
             to the sound of mosquitoes

      electrocuted on the aluminum Pest-Rid machine.

The Grace of a Monday Evening

At home my wife was chopping salad, talking to herself, something about tectonic plates that rive continents and make oceans. I just came out with it. "I banged Grace," I said, "in the baptismal font."

My wife spun. "You mean grace," she said, "as in *gratia*, from Latin, meaning good will, gratitude?"

"Yes! Grace," I cried, "as in absolution, mercy for a life well lived."

She held me in her arms. The sun was setting. We stood trembling in the jonquil light. We were ecstatic. She whispered in my ear: "The sun! The sun! It's not even sinking below the rooftops, as it seems to be."

"It's stationary!" I yelled, perhaps too loud.

"It's us that fly," she said, holding my arms as if I might float off.

"Glued," I said, "to this massive spinning rock, hurtling through space."

"It's unthinkable!" she said.

We kissed like babies.

A Cordial Letter from West Philadelphia

Kaylee Muthart, from Anderson, South Carolina made headlines when
she was rushed to the hospital after she was found tearing her own
eyes out in front of a church . . . Now, completely blind but drug-free,
the 20-year-old says . . . "Life's more beautiful now, life's more beautiful
than it was being on drugs. It is a horrible world to live in."
        —*THE INDEPENDENT* (11 MARCH 2018)

Kaylee, do you ever feel,
now blind and off the meth,
            like a sunflower in a vase?

Uprooted, I mean.
I do! I'll try my best
            to tell you what I see.

I'm in Clark Park, sunny spring day.
Trees, picnickers, squirrels.
            How can I enact

these row homes for you?
Their silent façades
            tremble with familiarity.

That's no good. The trembling
is a trolley rolling by.
            And on the wind

a whiff of the end of the world.
You smell it, too, I bet.
            Let me try again.

These robins! A bush
of screaming prophets.
            Can you feel my relief?

I'm bad at this. How can I portray
this woozy circus music
            ice cream truck?

How can I animate the earth
so you'll see it, too? Long ago,
            when I arrived at the page,

the words were there for me,
first graders waiting in line;
            now they glower, goblins

in dark potholes. They owe me nothing
and know it. How I long for you
            to see Clark Park!

The men playing chess, the girl
and her grandma handing a popsicle
            back and forth. I'm here, Kaylee,

dead center of the universe,
I swear. As if we, all of us,
            were emerging from a coma.

The way this homeless fella,
straw hat, elastic under his chin,
            trembles in the grass. The way

I trembled during my first kiss.
That was winter. Linda,
            short, red-haired Linda,

rolled onto me in the snow.
That weight. Lips warm.
                    So now, the world emerging,

        we are free to name the things
in it. *This* wind, *that* leaf.
                    This hand of mine

        which is a kind of begging bowl.
The moment of transgression
                    and fog has passed.

        It's just you and me, Kaylee,
in this horrible clarity. Can you
                    believe there's a word

        for every item in the park?
The *straw hat*. The *popsicle*.
                    Everything nameable.

        Even that kiss, Linda urging
my head into the snow,
                    I'd call *beautiful*.

Amateur Escapologists

"I love you, Mandy," I said, kissing her belly button.

"Brandy," she said.

"Tell me everything, Brandy," I said.

"I have a kid named Kandy," she said. She showed me a photo of a tomboy in a striped baseball cap, big smile, front tooth missing.

"Leave her. Run away with me," I said.

Brandy cried and cried. We climbed on a bus.

For years we lived in harmony. Brandy delivered mail for the post office. I waited tables at a diner. Each evening we met at the diner for burgers. We sat in a booth and read letters Brandy had stolen. I held up a foolscap page teeming with tight purple loops and read, "With you I climax with such outrage as to stitch a fissure in the drum-pulse of the earth." We laughed and tore it to bits. Brandy found a greeting card. "HAPPY BIRTHDAY," it said. Inside was written, in wobbly old-world script, "You are quite unnecessary, young man!" A ten-dollar bill floated out. We ordered milkshakes. Then Brandy was sobbing, holding an envelope that said "Toof Ferry."

We climbed on a bus. Kandy lived in a tiny unpainted house at the edge of town, near a tent city of homeless vets. Brandy banged on the door. Brandy answered: not a twin, it was *her*. Same eyes, hair, everything. Brandy stared at Brandy. Brandy said, "Have you heard the roar of the sea?" Brandy replied, "The woods are riddled with paths, untold ways out." They hugged. My Brandy walked in, calling, "Kandy-cane!" The other Brandy walked out, kissing me softly.

Brandy and I hopped the fence and walked through the derelict village of vets toward the bus station.

The First Movie Star

The dame in the fruit hat
watching her own flicks: "I'd no *idea*,"
   patting ash-blonde hair,
"so many people were interested

   in me." Who is that lady,
pretty eagle-beak nose, cleft chin?
   Florence Lawrence,
household name. 1914,

   filming *Pawns of Destiny,*
she caught fire. A staged blaze
   slipped its handcuffs.
Ever looked fire in the face?

   It's white, red, black, gray.
Knife-in-a-light-socket *white*.
   Van-Gogh's-*Red-Vineyard red*.
Moth-on-your-wrist *gray*.

   Black and white film
—as in the flaming-tree scene
   of *The Maelstrom*
where Lawrence slays

   as a puckish mermaid—
renders fire white, gray, black, gray.
   Lawrence, paralyzed,
bedridden. Months later

   she stormed back on set,
slapped a hospital bill on
   the producer's desk,
ready to act. *Hell yeah!* But

she who'd been lovely, pale,
pink outside and in,
    now had a long red scar
under her chin, a pancreas-shaped

    blotch on her cheek.
Gunfire floored Archduke Ferdinand.
    There came a fusillade
of bodies, one torching the next,

    human kindling, and in the throats
of generals in horned hats,
    carnal sparks. The career of Florence
Lawrence, pale at the bottom,

    grayed. Flops, uncredited. Scenes
deleted. Divorced, childless.
    Penniless. There is a Siamese cat,
gift of Fatty Arbuckle.

    There are Pall Malls,
high heels. Stacks of fan mail
    under faint electric light.
Late one night, she mixes

    ant paste with cough syrup,
licks it off her thumb.
    A fat hand wipes cigar ash
off a big red corny heart-shaped desk.

A Self-Guided Tour of Machu Picchu, or Please, Sir/Madam, Step Away from the Edge of the Abyss

A squat old US tourist with big thick 1950s movie-mogul glasses
stumbles 400 feet. It takes an hour to climb
                    steep stone steps the Incas carved

or just seconds to topple down them headfirst
as this Argentine in a green velvet cape does.
                    Beware overgrown cliffside paths!

Bosque nuboso, cloud forests, run from tropical lowlands
up to the Incan citadel, at whose summit
                    in a charming high-altitude thicket

a Russian tourist is torched by lightning.
Our suffering bodies, unlike poems, are ignoble, ungainly.
                    The eastern slopes contain

a rich biodiversity. And *crazy* views. Look,
a Spanish tourist's heart just stops—
                    lottery ticket in his pocket. (Winner?

It is *not.*) True! All true! I swear by the water mirrors
of Inti Mach'ay cave, where a tourist
                    (Danish, mullet, guidebook opened

to the Royal Feast of the Sun) is having a cardiac event—
in his pocket in a tiny Ziploc bag,
                    his mother's stirrup-shaped

throat bone. Sure I believe in
the blessedness of human life
                    but sometimes Jesus Christ

a belly laugh bounds forth unawares,
as the graceful tourist streakers who
            to the dismay of Peruvian officials

bound naked as elk over the grasslands.
From time immemorial the stones
            of Inti Watana have pointed

toward the sun in winter solstice.
A rock falls on a German couple: the boy, plummeting
            down the slope, emits a sound of—

But I shouldn't. Some words you write,
cross out, and never tell anyone,
            like ever. The high priest and local virgins

lived at the peak of Huayna Picchu.
A Belgian man with bad eyesight
            climbs to where the Urubamba River bends,

drops clean off. Do not smirk.
How must we look to him in that fold of time?
            What Flemish expletive

does he blurt out? A German tourist
asks a stranger to snap a photo of him
            midair: he jumps, slips off the cliff.

A park ranger explains:
"He was at the edge with his back to the abyss.
            Many tourists from all over,

especially foreigners, always get very close
to the edge of the abysses."
   El borde de los abismos.

   Is this why Neruda calls Machu Picchu
"Inaccessible storm sealed off"?
      Oh not just storm,

   witch in a storm, eyes broken stones,
locking eyes with you, an inaccessible
         light an abysmal light she cries

   Hallelujah! whose ending *yah*
from Hebrew Yahweh means
      Mother o mother fuck I am dying!

The Deer of Philadelphia

I was carrying the limp corpse of a white-tailed doe over my back down Broad Street, her legs swinging around my ears. I dragged my feet: she weighed about the same as my father.

A little girl hopped past: a deer with bright velvet antlers skipped beside her. Cars were stopped at a red light. Variegated deer grazed and leapt among the vehicles and pedestrians on their way to lunch. It gave the street an ethereal look, as if it were dusk and not midday.

In front of a deli, an unusual deer—light blue, almost invisible, with tall ears, black tail—was sniffing each thing: bench, trash can, even a mime with a bouquet of imaginary flowers, then recoiling from noisy jackhammers. She sniffed me impassively. This was, I knew, Frody's deer.

And there was Frody. "Frody! Frody!" I cried, shifting my deer from one shoulder to the other. Frody smiled cautiously. My fingers trembled. I'd anticipated this moment. "All my life I've made mistakes—" I started, as Frody's eyes strayed to his deer, which was weaving amid the taxis. "But *you,* Frody. You are my real, real, real, real…"

The word I sought floated out of reach. A plastic bag drifted upward, drawn into the wake of the deer trotting back and forth. Frody touched his forehead to my forehead and walked off toward his deer. As I turned away, I felt my dead deer craning to catch a last glimpse of Frody.

Resurrection Walk

I'm walking, almost skipping, up Sansom
past the noshery, suddenly this broad moon
of a face, brown hair, freckles, hard beauty,
so I stop,
        step back, backward, slow at first,
a few steps, not to trip,
               then briskly, back, back,
toward the bridge, up the Schuylkill, back
I step, along the highway, toe-heel, toe-heel,
always backward, shoulder of the road,
vehicles hissing by, sports car, minivan,
transport truck,
           hours pass, days, weeks,
sun rising west, setting east, I see
wrong-way-round to what's behind, what's gone,
roadkill twisting in a blood sunhat
toward a pickup truck, then it pops up,
the skunk, trotting backward
into a grove,
          summer folds into spring,
spring to winter, flowers shrink, green wanes,
kids put on sweaters, mufflers, hoods,
old folks
        pick up speed, I walk on,
back, back, toe-heel, toe-heel, my grandma
hops out of her wheelchair, walks unaided
backward into her Inwood apartment,
waving, Hallo, Hallo, a sheet is lifted
from Matthew's body, his face
convulsing, frowning, he flips me the bird,
leaps backward into his painting studio,
a box is lifted
        out of the ground, lid removed,

Zoë is hoisted into a black car that backs away
to the morgue, ICU, bed, Zoë chokes
awake, eyelids twitch, fingers shiver, lifted
onto a gurney and backed out of the hospital
into an ambulance, to a park, lowered
onto the street in a heap from which
she springs suddenly uncoiling into the air
spiraling roadgashed toward a Toyota,
wounds closing, her moth-wing ribcage
against the wind-
                           shield, and Zoë rises
backward smoothly onto her feet
into a rhythmic run, evening sun climbing,
Toyota speeding in reverse through
the broken fence, away from Zoë who jogs
back, up the stairs, toe, toe, toe, toe,
freckles, nose ring, earbuds, the Toyota
swerves backward
                           out of the park
to a pub, spits a man onto a stool
vomiting drink after drink
out of his stomach into a glass.

The Great Cooling

When you pass on, our excitement
about you—how else to put it?
                    —cools. Like a house party

when the cops arrive:
lights thrown on, drugs flushed,
                    guests scattered.

The excitement we felt
at the airport gate when
                    you returned from the war.

Why we exclaimed, "At last!"
when you came out of the closet.
                    How we wept at your birth!

And when you became a wife,
father, grandmother,
                    prizewinner. *Cools.*

Even when you needed
forgiving, running manic
                    in the hospital,

or lying on our kitchen floor,
a kind of feral dog. Even then
                    you thrilled us!

But when you die—we can't help it—
the thrill cools. Like a porn star's
                    mustache in the rain.

I will never love Rembrandt
the way I love Tiina.
             After all, Tiina breathes—

Rembrandt is just oils
and magic. But when Tiina goes,
             it might have been better

if she'd been a painting all along.
When I go, my force—
             which you understood

from my dancing
more than my poems—
             dissipates. To Newton,

the rate an object cools
is proportional to the difference
             in temperature between

the object and its surroundings.
You, the dead one, are the object;
             we, your surroundings.

Our heat goes up, briefly,
then (matching how cold
             you have become) down;

and as we forget you,
up again, and so on.
             When Matthew decided

to step away from us,
I stomped across West Philly,
              mind a hill of fire ants.

     I wept on the phone
with his mother. Wrote poem after poem.
          It passed.

     Some grief remains in the gut,
bad meat, perhaps forever. But
          that stomping and crying

     is the last excitement
anyone will feel
          for you. Ever!

Impossible Household

Jill and I kept no secrets.
We spoke everything out loud
like toddlers. One day
out of pure boredom
I told a lie. As I said it, my voice
creaked, a rotten stair.
Jill noticed, smiled.

That lie was so fun,
I did it again. Secrets collected.
I buried them in the yard.
Watching the sunset with Jill,
it was hard to pretend
not to notice the mounds of dirt,
wasps flying out of them,
swarming us.

I admired Jill's honesty
but when she died I found,
in her jeans pocket,
a map to her island of secrets.
Next day at noon,
I stepped off the ferry.

Villagers spoke of a statue
of a traumatized, bed-wetting girl.
In the abandoned school,
rooms of gas masks,
disintegrating desks,
one tennis sneaker
on a pillow of needles.
No statue.

Below a Ferris wheel
overgrown with wildflowers:
Joan of Arc, in the flesh,
with Jill's face. Is that you,
she said, Son of Man?

Yes, I cried, it's me!
We hugged and sat
and talked all night.
We confessed our lies
and wept as we parted.

In the morning
the humble boatman
ferrying travelers
across the stormy waters
told me to go fuck myself.

I swam to the coast,
emerging naked on the sand,
my skin giving off
a minute light.

Twilight in the English Department

The student stepped in without a word and sat bolt upright, just as I was sitting, across the swamp of papers, nodding as I did, mirroring each of my gestures. "Welcome, my boy," I said. "Excuse my labyrinthine chamber of—"

"Please, sir!" he said. "I've lost something crucial."

I assumed he was referring to the F I awarded him for his last essay. "What's wrong?" I said, leaning back in my chair, slow.

He, too, leaned back. "My son," he said, "doesn't know me." We sat in silence, staring at each other in the darkening office.

"Father!" I shouted.

The Archaic Tower of John Alan Barger

for my father

The bottom floors
now flimsy
collapse. Long ago a zoo
with animals clean and unclean
commingled in cages
of gopher wood
smeared with pitch.

An underground parking garage
heaped with megafauna
skeletons resembling
a giant's broken furniture.

In the lobby
lunatics feast on scattered
plaster and rats,
speaking nicknames of God.

Thirty floors up at the penitentiary
the structure broadens.
Inmates wash corpses
(*whose* corpses?), feeding them
into a furnace
that fuels the tower.

Above, a museum. Floor after floor
of tiny shrunken boys,
delinquents in black jackets
preserved in jars. Ornate rooms,
entablatures, scrawlings.
Double-locked, deserted.

The penthouse, once elegant,
now pockmarked
by sun, hail, years.

Fog veils the highest floors.

Hard to know
how high it goes.
Accounts are cloaked in fable.

Visitors, they say,
must row a dark body of water
to hills of wolves
or wiseacres in faux fur
that fall upon you
snarling.

Self-Harm Song

Once, on the afternoon we met,
a woman showed me her upper thigh.
Deep red rivers across it. She lives,
she explained, in the black stream
beneath perfection. "What," she said,
"cut if not yourself?" Such a release.
It just feels right. Some of us *barber*
ourselves, as show mice do,
nipping our fur till it peels off
like a hay roof in a hurricane.
Some caged birds pluck their
feathers, mutilate their skin.
You sense as the knife sinks in
the ancient laughter howl of outrage
pulsebeat of the world. It hurts
but is honest. Sid Vicious knew it.
Eunuch priests, too, self-flagellating
on the day of blood, *Dies Sanguinis,*
eyes rolling in fever-dream parodies of Christ.
O self-harm goddess, part phoenix,
chained and flaming, your touch
a cataclysm, your heart a crucifixion.
Chimera of humiliation, release us!
She responds, "Daughters, sons, *other ones*—
to crack the egg of the hidden island,
turn your shame *inward.*"
So that's what we tell our fledglings
with every wink and poke.
We can't soothe them, or ourselves.
Instead, we—waving, laughing, thumbs up—
trot you out of doors in bright dresses
and ironed shirts, into the sunlight,
alone. I had a bandy-legged dog,

she got so distraught when I went out
she licked her paw to the bone.
She meant no harm, it was just love
she didn't know where to put.

The Dog Catcher's Boy

Hungover in the pizza aisle I hear, "You fat lazy fuck-tard!" A
mother to her small son. Behind her he toddles, in overalls,
tiny gravy boat. She yanks his ear, too hard. My gorge rises. Fie!
O, to roll off with the boy in my cart, past the watermelons to
the street, pressing his doughy cheek to mine.

I'd care for the little guy. He'd join me each morning in my
milk truck. No, *dog catcher* truck. I'd show him how, with a
burlap sack and a hot dog, to catch any dog in town. "Cast your
net wide, son," I tell him and for a few good years it's all pillow
fights and cookie dough. Then he gets married.

One afternoon I follow a ragged shivering Rottweiler under
a bridge that doesn't exist. I'm on my back in a bouquet of ether
and iodine. A ventilator—tic *hisss,* tic *hisss*—forces air in and
out of my lungs. My boy weeps on his wife's shoulder. She shuts
the door, nods at him. He unplugs the machine.

"Now, finally," she whispers, "the dogs will be *free.*"

Insomniac in Center City

I climb aboard the trolley like a Madagascan
fat-tailed dwarf lemur, which hibernates
six months, vanishing into sleep
half his life. *Lemures* (Latin): spirits of the dead
roaming at a slow pace. Humans sleep
twenty-five years. I sleep so little,
it's as if I'm always sleeping. Look,
it's snowing on the dogs of Clark Park.
A cow can sleep standing up but only dreams
lying down. The Oaxaca cave sleeper fish
has no eyes. Does it dream? To locate
sustenance in a nutrient-poor environment,
it veers toward vibrations. As I am a poet
in Philadelphia, this resonates. Bone-weary
on the packed trolley, I stand, bovine.
With each blink I dream. On Market Street,
circadian lopsidedness. A man in a tin-foil hat
shrieks. I, extra in a school play, step out
of the frame. Shut my eyes. After a day,
insomniacs nod off. A few seconds at first.
I'm jarred awake by a brass band, North Broad.
Look, in the snow, among the cars,
two men on horses. I veer toward them.
I hop on a horse, roaming at a nice slow pace
across a parking lot, under a bridge.
A cop waves to me. An addict waves
from inside a garbage-bag tent. The mayor
waves, drapes his sash around my neck.
Snow is rising to my horse's knees. Who cares?
Now I'm the mayor of Broad Street. The mayor of snow.

You Were Scheduled to Duel with Elvis Presley

At cockcrow a proxy jogs up
    wheezing, sweating,
waving a note from The King.
    Let's call the proxy
Colonel Tom Parker.
    Birds sing. A pretty morning.
You and Colonel Tom Parker
    sit in the grass
under an apple tree.
    He unfolds the note.
An illegible scrawl,
    orange crayon,
maybe a drawing of a tiger.
    The Colonel beams,
watching your face.
    In the violet light
his face is round, genial.
    Black bolo tie,
white cowboy hat.
    Maybe the Colonel
will be your new friend.
    He knows people,
he says. Stick with him,
    you'll go places.
You holster your pistol.
    "Folks such as yourself,"
he says, "*decent* folks,
    are a kind of grace
God bestows on this world."
    With veneration
he offers you an orange
    clown wig. You put it on.

"You're a natural!"
    he squeals, squinting for
an unseeable camera.
    So your future uncoils,
inevitable, necessary.
    A herd of goats
upright on their hind legs
    totters by, ungainly
and with great pomp:
    skeletal saints.

Three Photos of Jayne Mansfield

First photo:
Mansfield laid out beside a car wreck,
    top of her head missing.
A journalist, finding her blonde wig,

    said she'd been beheaded.
At 2:25 a.m., an insecticide truck
    had come barreling
in a cloud of chemicals. The impact

    sliced the roof of Mansfield's car,
a 1966 Buick Electra, clean off.
    Of four Chihuahuas, just one died.
Second photo: Mansfield,

    beside Sophia Loren
at a fancy Hollywood dinner,
    allows her breasts to cascade
out of her silky dress. Loren

    is aghast. The two men beside Loren
are having an awful night.
    Mansfield, gorgeous Mansfield,
is a wreck. Nobody looks happy

    in either pic. The first
is overexposed, the star's corpse
    a mottled lump on the bright white
shoulder of the road,

    the deep black night a fog encroaching.
It's beautiful, I mean. Transcendent.
    The other day a friend of mine
suggested that civilization is just

an elaborate design to cover up shit.
I thought of *you,* Jayne Mansfield,
   how the end confirms
what we already knew.

   When the wig of life is yanked off,
we see the truth. We are jealous,
   righteous, malicious,
having suspected your ugliness.

   When beauty ends,
we aren't surprised or let down.
   The opposite. We hold
the bloody blonde wig in our hands.

   We try it on, look in the mirror.
We preen, all of us, divas for a moment.
   This is the third photo.
The same, exactly, as the other two.

The Resurrectionist

Police say they have no clues to the grave robbers who stole
Charlie Chaplin's body from a small, unguarded Swiss village
cemetery two nights ago.

—*ASSOCIATED PRESS* (MARCH 3, 1978)

They dragged the coffin to their shack. The squat, toad-faced
goon collapsed, dog-tired.

The lanky one, alone with the body, giggled.

He flipped on the TV. *Modern Times!* Of the two, he was the
soft touch. Ticklish. Hypochondriac. A grin from a broad made
his grog blossoms glow.

Hearing his pal snore, he peeked into the box and, seeing
the burst old man, paused. The face flesh quivered, gray orzo.
He removed his bowler hat and lowered it onto the skull.
Squinted, trying to picture the famous mustache.

A spring gale rattled the windows. Suddenly, what had
seemed like many things was only this.

IV

The Effluvial Repentance of Samuel Sewall

Sewall, a judge at the 1692 Salem witchcraft trials,
killed women. Sewage—from Old French *essouier,*
          "to drain"—is released to waterways

     such as rivers flowing to seas.
A ghoulish, fire-breathing judge.
               In a sedimentation tank,

     fecal sludge is pumped, bacteria
dried, detoxified. Processed, treated,
               purified. Sewall, in puritanical plumage,

     fluent in the ruinous vernacular,
condemned twenty to death by hanging.
               Any remaining organic material

     dissolves in the effluent. Five years later,
Sewell repented, admitting
               he was wrong. Which is called humus.

     In 1718, he was appointed Chief Justice
of the Superior Court of Judicature.
               In these tanks, solids sink

     to the bottom. In his old age,
he denounced slavery. Enslaved people, he wrote,
               ought to be treated

     with a Respect agreeable.
Sewage can be used to run your car,
               make hydroelectric power,

methane. World history a draining.
So then, saith the Son of Man,
    because thou art lukewarm,

  and neither cold nor hot, I will spue thee
out of my mouth. An eruption,
    regurgitation. It can even power

  cellphones. A flood. Sewall
considered himself more at fault than others.
    Fecal bacteria

  may occur in ambient water
as a result of the overflow of domestic sewage.
    No other Salem judge

  had a change of heart. Trace
amounts of feces exist in
    all water on earth.

The Hole in My Backyard

I get very nervous, I admit. If I take a day off to relax, tension drifts out my nose: a kind of thin mist. It doesn't go far, the tension. It remains seated politely on the couch beside me, in the form of a ghost I call Marcus Aurelius.

Marcus Aurelius and I sit in the yard gossiping, as evening shadows lengthen. He is wise and knows things about the neighbors. Alex walks past, waves. Marcus Aurelius and I wave back. I say, "Alex looks dapper in his red suspenders." Marcus Aurelius nods and says, "Did you know that Alex intends to hang himself today?" No, I did not.

On a lark, and because he is magic, I ask Marcus Aurelius if he wouldn't mind venturing down into the hole in my backyard. He agrees without asking which hole. He knows I mean the one I wanted to dig when I was a kid, but my parents wouldn't let me. It was going to be a point of refuge, a safe place, for when trouble visited the house. Although there is no hole, Marcus Aurelius steps down into it, silent and dignified.

I peek into Mrs. Kaulback's kitchen. She leans her forehead on the window to watch her cats mill in the grass: imperious, doomed titans.

Marcus Aurelius is back, gazing up at the sky. "Man, it's beautiful down there," he says. "No way," I say. "Oh yeah," he says. "Like Machu Picchu," he says. Apparently the more he sat in the hole, the more he wanted to be a better person. I love it when he talks like that.

"What are you fellows chatting about?" says Alex's ghost. "The hole in John's backyard," says Marcus Aurelius. Without a word, Alex's ghost steps down into the hole.

He leaves behind a deep serenity in the backyard, interrupted just once by Mrs. Kaulback moving furniture. Or it might have been a peal of thunder.

First Consultation with the Plastic Surgeon

Oh—! Did I disturb your face
as it was performing a double somersault?
This face of yours has thrown
tantrums. Of course it has!
Any face that hasn't
is a wee cold moon. Ha, ha.
You like that one? You like *wee?*
Me too. Let's open this book
of wee faces. Look at *this* face.
Is *this* the face you want?
Here is a face that glows
in starlight. Here is a face
that cannot be exhausted by use.
You think, *heh,* your face glows
in starlight? Think your face
is an exotic circus animal
that forgot its tricks?
Seriously now. Your face
is a dogfight. A malevolent
fairy tale. Seriously. Your eyes
subzero spotlights in your head.
Who'd enter such a face
to brave the Minotaur within?
Look at *this* face. This pretty
face, here: wolves of poverty
devoured the cheeks,
fish of bereavement the eyes.
Discard the one, take the other.
The greatest cutting does not sever.
Look at *this* face: "Truthful,"
Keats might have said.
He was wrong. Beauty and Truth
are antithetical. The secret

of a face is it has no secrets?
Wrong. A face is the secret
of a heart. Heart the secret
of a soul. Soul the secret
of God. In my nightmare
the faces are impassive, bleak:
icebergs unmelting. Let the river
of *your* face jump its banks.
Let the animals of your face
run into the light and let them fall.

A Sprout Is the Disintegration of the Seed

Every night we are afraid
we shut our eyes
we reveal ourselves
to the night
and to our blankets
as the dwarves of Auschwitz
were revealed
to Josef Mengele.

They took us
from the orphanage
in a dump truck
backed up to a fire pit,
we tumbled out,
Josef Mengele and the SS officers
burst out of the forest
on motorcycles
circling the flames.
To each other we call him
Angel of Death.
As he straps me
to his table he is civil.
He chats, he smiles.
I shut my eyes.

Ugliness is a disease,
he chirps. He cuts
with a surprisingly
light touch. Death
is just nature, he says.
Beauty is . . . *more.*
He isn't bothered
much. He cuts, he cuts.

He chuckles to a nurse—
Do you think I resemble
Hemingway? Is a sprout
the disintegratedness
of the seed? Would *you*
like to walk as a hermit crab?
I do not know what to say.
He's chatting away—
sawing my legs,
needle after needle
in my ear. My body a forge
and he is Hephaestus.
His eyes a blue sea
and the brown-eyed Jew
(he sings) a ship upon it.

You want to know
why I whistled
while I worked.
I *liked* cleft lips
and chins. I liked twins,
symmetry. Who
doesn't like beauty?
Do you like to ski?
After the war I skied
with Rolf, my son,
in Switzerland.
I was Onkel Fritz
to him. He was young,
what did he know?

At the café, a dwarf
brought tea and lebkuchen.

The dwarf, a chatty one,
asked, "Fun day
with dad, *mäuschen?*"
Rolf looked at me
with pity, said to the waiter,
"Father was a *hero,*
you fucking goblin."

What Happened in Savona

Why's our train stopped
the purring behemoth breathing its steam
            what portent

            its long shadows on the platform
will befall us, o we marvelous
            commuters, outraged commuters

            shrilling into our phones
what wonder, what sign, what epistemology, what—
            a conductor says

            someone leapt on the tracks,
is alive—*alive?*
            —a scene in *De Humani Corporis*

            Fabrica, a hospital, a dolly shot
follows two old women walking down a hall
            screams growing

            from *elsewhere*
maybe a cat, piercing, screeching,
            over and over the screams,

            the camera seeks out
the source, turns a corner, turns a corner,
            finally the camera, steady, says *this,*

            this is the source,
a woman huddled, cornered,
            on the verge of—

screaming into the camera,
at us, o nameless fragile
            self-hurting

    scared little thing, o Ligurian suicide,
there's no word or paraphrase
                for these falling coins

    of dusk (I inhale
deeply) dissolving
                as ink in water,

    for being alive today, here,
in this terrifying (I feel it)
                tiny spider-sized moment of

Did We Not Say

Did we not say
there is pain every night?

To be clear, you will fall asleep
in the village *every night*
holding a lit match,
your soul a birthing canal
in cold night wind.

The lit match a blue note
over a page. Oh man,
it will feel good
to drop the match.
But the sheer power
of holding it.
The sheer flower
of dropping it. It will feel
sheer, dropping it.
It will feel lit.
Such levitation.

This page.

Child, wring yourself
clean as a sock.
That's how I'd do it.
Can you not see the char
of the village?
The char it will be?
The faint pong
of turpentine it will be?

Burn the village.

And when suddenly
there is too much beauty,
burn it. And when
a trap door in the night opens,
fall through it.

Epoch of The Babies

One day they just stepped
out of the forest behind the mall.
We pointed and laughed
at their huge eyes, bland faces.
We called them *The Babies.*
They didn't mind. They called us
Mothers. They were polite.
Hugging our women, bowing to
our men. Fuck them, we said,
their creaseless faces and genuflections.
We couldn't bear it. We humiliated them.
Exiled, hunted them. Hanged them
from stoplights. The Babies
fought back. Rolled over us
with our machines. Occupied city hall.
There was a Baby in every kitchen.
We turned on each other.
Each family harbored a traitor.
Buses marked "Reeducation Camps"
lined our streets. Our mayor wandered
the road, naked, weeping. Three Babies
smashed our door, walked us
through a cornfield under the moon.
My wife, wiping our son's cheek,
kept slipping in the mud. A bus idled,
packed. Across the side, a banner:
"MOTHER'S LIGHT WAS NOT HEREDITARY."
To me a Baby whispered, not unkindly,
"Mother, you glitter with what you have done."
All night the loudspeakers blared:
"Mother, Mother, we revered you as gods..."
And then, as our bus pulled away:
"Mother, mother, mother, mother, mother, mother..."

Three Beautiful Heart Attacks

I barely glimpsed her—
she was sniffing a pineapple
at the grocery store:
black swan under an El Greco storm cloud.

I woke in a hospital,
dearth and famine
of the world upon me,
and was released into a taxi.

Over and over I pictured her,
the surging inner sea
of her sniffing the pineapple.
To such a man as I had become
everything resembles truth.
Anything can happen.

Next, at a museum,
she was looking at a human skeleton
riding a horse skeleton,
her yellow dress
holding the world together.

I woke in a hospital,
doctor frowning.
Avoid all stress, she said,
and take these pills.

I drove to the airport,
sat at my gate, gaze lowered.

From the corner of my eye,
bare feet on a red suitcase.
Silence shivered.
An oak tree of silence inside me.

Nagasaki Tree

At the sun-bright hypocenter
of the blast, a big ol'
barnacled bride of a camphor tree
held, scorched bald,
deaf as a dandelion.
At Mitsubishi Steel,
girders bent, limp, jellified.
A year later the tree drooled,
hulking in its burnt pasture,
manacled beast. That spring
—gasping, a fish tossed back
in the sea—its buds erupt
magnanimously,
a sweeping gesture of the boughs
suggesting a vast world
beyond the parking lot.
Still today it stands
tarred in place, braced
with cord, scarves in its hair,
stooped, warty,
badass. A boxer, punched
square in the jaw,
can lose consciousness
a split second (in the dream
I slip into lake water
with *her,* the dead friend).
They return petrified,
swinging like gods.

The World-Ending Fox

I was a hermit on a mountain
   doing my chores,
one eye on the village below.
   This morning the villagers
outside their factory
   under the smokestack
were shouting, shaking their fists.
   As I washed my clothes,
the orange-faced mayor
   rolled up in a black car.
He pointed and the blacklegs
   sprayed the townsfolk
with rust-colored gas. It was tricky,
   beating my pants on a rock,
to have an opinion of this:
   you can bet both sides
had their reasons. I sang along
   with the birds in the long
morning, while coppery mist
   choked the villagers.
I saw them hurling bricks
   and heard, dimly,
their coughing and furious
   howls. These sounds mingled
with another: a *hissing,* nearby.
   Thunderous sibilance.
The earth vibrated. I followed it,
   the sound, to its source:
a leafless oak tree. Under the tree
   sat a fox going "*Sssssssss-
sssssssss…*" The mountain quieted.
   I thought to myself, I thought,
this here fox be sucking

all sound out of the world.
I asked the fox, "Prithee,
    won't objects *follow* their sound?"
The fox just sat under the tree
    hissing. I asked the fox,
"You a world-ending fox?"
    But the fox just hissed. The fox
just hissed and the rusty gas lifted,
    and the leaves on the trees
lifted, and my tumbledown cabin lifted
    so the mountain looked smaller.
Thunderous, the sound.
    When I saw the birds were gone
I let the pants go, the ones
    I'd been gripping. In truth,
mister man, there wasn't time for awe,
    it simply happened, just like that,
a kind of screen door latching.
    And as I felt my body ebbing,
lessening, I thought to myself,
    I thought, while I do enjoy
my tumbledown cabin and my trees
    and my quiet times, you can bet
there are *reasons* why this fox has come,
    well beyond my knowing.
It was the sound of an anchor chain,
    the kind that moors ships,
paying out link by link through the top
    of the skull, up and up and up.

The World According to Li'l _____

Schoolkids in bright uniforms ran down the steps to the street. One stopped to stare at me. Li'l _____, son of a boy to whom I'd given a nickname so cruel, it immediately stuck and became his only name. His mother called him in at dusk using the name. His wife, in bed, whispered the name in his ear. He passed the name on to his only son.

And last year he hanged himself, I read.

Li'l _____ hopped up to me like a bird, overbite, smiling. The basketball he held was so clean it looked as if it had never touched the ground. He looked me over. "If your body i*th* not healthy," he lisped, "your *th*oul can overcome it."

I grinned. "Is my body unhealthy?"

"In th' name of Yahweh, ye*th*."

I laughed in his face. "What is Yahweh, Li'l _____?"

He gestured to the glass buildings around us: "If tho*the* mountains had eye*th*, they would be Yahweh'*th* face."

"What does your Yahweh say about *loss*, kid?" As I said this, I rolled his ball down the road, into traffic.

He looked at me a long time. I felt the river of my belly freezing over. My cheeks wet with tears. The streetlights ignited: multitudinous buds. I don't know how long he'd been holding my hand.

The Lighthouse

I

The shore shifts, variable, receding, dispersing, toward sea, toward land, toward sky

In the four directions the shore shifts, dilates, climbs, lopes, shivers

A lighthouse by its nature warns against a rocky shore

Sorrowful, pale, spectral lighthouse, immense lighthouse above the city

We citizens below ask, What variable shore *in us* called out for such a structure of pale sorrow, and for such light?

Were we out to sea? Where is the land?

And, friends, where is the lighthouse?

We turned, the lighthouse was gone. Was it blown down?

O sentinel, pencil, daffodil whose color opens outward from the middle

O beacon blazing such ecstatic lavender light—*yesterday!*

And, then, there it was again—*Look!*—in the main square of our city, our beloved city

No longer on the shore

There, beside you! And you act as though you can't see it!

II

Friends, I am so small compared to you. The very smallest thing in the city

All I see is the lighthouse. It fills my eyes. Under the lighthouse in the wind
I am most alive, a candle sputtering

All of my laughter, my mirth, a part of it

Just as its light is part of the stars, though not a reflection of them

The lighthouse emanates its own light

See how the sky around it glows lavender at dusk?

In truth, between you and me, I don't see the lighthouse either anymore

We all knew where it was until we didn't

Then it was gone one hundred years. Nobody—not even fanatics, lunatics,
politicians—saw it

At a certain point, to see the lighthouse was "a miracle"

To this hour women in rags frail as damselflies walk the city blocks seeking
the lighthouse whispering I am the bride I am the bride of the lighthouse

It became a superstition, tourist ploy. We sold pewter lighthouses, keychain
lighthouses, grandfather clock lighthouses

We sold a paper lighthouse, called the Ghost Pharos, to set aflame at your
wake to assure a lighthouse in the afterlife

Until, pondering the lighthouse, a huge tiredness came over you

As when you hold a sparrow in your mouth that still sings, but less, less. Then the sparrow (still in your mouth) does not sing for a century

III

The groom waits at the altar, they prophesied. The teacher is nigh, they assured us

And lo, there it was again. Miracle tower, lodestar, lighthouse!

Had it been laid low by a gale? Who rebuilt it? No one asked. We were happy. We danced, sang, hands in the air

At night, still the shore shifts

Look, *there,* a woman climbing the lighthouse! She yells down to us—a warning, or curse—then plunges upon the jagged sea wall

I collect her body, offer it to the lighthouse

Melancholy and joyous, I suddenly know my place

Friends! I, lowly lighthead, am the one creature qualified to observe with certainty how beautiful you are

You who lean over this poem, craving the dim lavender flame

I care about no other thing than to notice you, to *see* you

I circle the lighthouse repeating its myriad names in the summer of all dances

I, star-blind, heart-raw, turn to you, in love with you, your bioluminescence

Me, the Lighthouse Tender? Ha! I'm just a bee shouldering my suicide horn among the poppies

Unfit to carry the coattails of the groom of the lighthouse

IV

Some asked, Was the lighthouse *ever here?*

Although none of us had seen it, nor had our grandmothers' grandmothers, we formulated a stipulative definition for it, pending approval from city council

Difficult as it is to establish criteria for a miracle, we were confident we'd accomplished the task

Lighthouse (city/miracle, *stipulative*): 1) Our city, as all cities, is emblematic of a doctrine of salvation, manifest in the variable form of a lighthouse; 2) Our city incorporates a lighthouse, a feature found in all cities, visible to every citizen, even sightlessly, from windowless rooms; 3) Our city, as all cities, is itself a lighthouse whose every window glitters lavender

Addendum: The lighthouse a neck stretching below what head

Addendum: The lighthouse o sublime tree scattering fruit upon us starving birds

Addendum: The lighthouse a flickering lamp at the bedside of a wounded child

Thence, definition and addenda affixed on a plaque at city hall, we put the issue of the lighthouse to rest

But still the citizens, bearing torches on the cobblestones, spoke in hushed whispers

The lighthouse, they said, was no warning to avoid the coast but a siren calling acolytes to run their boats against it, to be drunk and in love with the variable coast shifting always like a fever dream

We split into two armed factions, butchering one another in the name of 1) The Divine Lavender that Fills Its Denizens with Bliss; 2) The Peacekeeping Lavender Mist that Immerses Its Denizens with Love

It was a civil war of tremendous violence

Such schisms bring me joy. I relish your struggles to the pith

V

A rooster wakes me. Look, *there,* a woman has been dancing all night—in pain, convulsive—below the lighthouse. Her skin emanates lavender light

The lighthouse a harp whose oceanic strumming I hear even with hands clamped over my ears

Whose light I see, eyes shut

I open my eyes, the lighthouse is gone. Every day it comes and goes. It is not capricious but lord knows I am

I don't remember its existence till I see it again and crack into tears

I pace around it speaking this poem like a head case

I am foraging for something at the foot of the lighthouse—but *what?*— among street dogs and weird flowers, and *ah*

I say to you (who craves, I know, I *see* you, the lavender flame, as I do), Do you see it?

And I clasp the sleeve of your shirt and say, *Do you see it?*

But you push past, brusquely

You who are preoccupied with some other lighthouse

The Resurrection of Eight Belles

The cheers for the winner's decisive victory were cut short when
Eight Belles, the runner-up, was euthanized on the track minutes
after the race when she collapsed with two broken front ankles.
　　—*ASSOCIATED PRESS* (MAY 11, 2008)

Galloping full tilt you fall
your legs broken
　　　　　hurling the jockey to the dirt.

I've seen the video.
You squirm at the feet of five men.
　　　　　The one in jeans, tan hat,

injects you where you lie
with potassium chloride.
　　　　　You, Eight Belles,

big shivering animal
yank at your straitjacket
　　　　　caged, raving before us

as if snakebit.
Meantime we sit
　　　　　in the stands

nibbling our pretzels,
not minding at all
　　　　　that you're gone.

For we *do* give.
We give all we can
　　　　　to the poor waifs overseas.

We burn palm branches
smear ash on our foreheads
              kneel on pillows.

    Then we turn you
into dog food.
            We render you.

    A poem, too, renders waste,
seeking its power. (*No,* not waste—
            not just waste.

    I mean blood. Suffering.)
So the clairvoyant bookies ask:
            After the dogs have eaten

    and the poem is read,
what relic remains?
            Each night on my walk

    beside the reservoir,
Eight Belles breaches,
            rearing, twisted,

    eyes roiling,
and splashes back
            into the water.

ACKNOWLEDGMENTS

My thanks to the editors of publications in which poems in this collection first appeared: *Able Muse, Arkansas Review, Asheville Poetry Review, BoomerLitMag, Burnside Review, Canadian Literature, The Cincinnati Review, Crannóg, A Dozen Nothing, Dunes Review, EVENT, The Fiddlehead, The Florida Review, I-70 Review, The Iowa Review, Lake Effect, The Missouri Review, Naugatuck River Review, Permafrost, Pleiades, Plume, Poetry Ireland Review, PRISM International, Rattle, River Styx, The Shoutflower, Sixth Finch, Smartish Pace, Tampa Review.*

Warm thanks to the team at LSU Press, especially my editor James W. Long for his guidance and encouragement. To the Canada Council for the Arts for assistance during crucial stages of this book. To Mary Dalton and series editor Anita Lahey for including "No Longer Invited to Dinner" in *Best Canadian Poetry 2026*. To Chase Twichell and her East Hill retreat, where some of this was written. To James Arthur, Jean Barger, Ben Gallagher, Warren C. Longmire, Cameron MacKenzie. And to Tiina.

www.ingramcontent.com/pod-product-compliance
Lightning Source LLC
Chambersburg PA
CBHW021543140426
43121CB00003BB/46